Escaping the Housework

Book Two

A Selection of Poems

By

Sylvia Charlewood

SpringwoodHouse Publishing

Escaping the Housework

Copyright Sylvia Charlewood 2014

First Published in the UK by SpringwoodHouse Publishing

12, Hillands Drive, Gloucestershire,GL53 9EU.

Other Titles in this Series:
Escaping the Housework 1 - Sylvia Charlewood

ISBN978-0-9929255-2-9

Dedication:

For My Family and Friends,

And to all those wonderful teachers, at the schools that I attended, at college and later at the Creative Writing Classes, who gave me insights, instructions, advice,and encouragement. And to my family who have always been so long-suffering, and who introduced me to the computer and its magic and especially to my son, without whose help and patience I could manage nothing. My sincere thanks, and my love, wherever they now are.

Table of Contents

1 -   Here there are no Rules

Here there are no rules – which is a blessing
I haven't got to go on guessing
what a 'modern' poem is –
 write thoughts unconnectedly;
I can be me: old-fashioned, iambic,
what I will; I can be free
to make such music as I can,
sing words out as they come to me.
There is no fence to tear, no barbed wire here
constraining what I feel
and see as real;
words come, bright, flowing in poetic light:
some are chaotic, unconnected,
some modest, delicate, collected
just as they are,
straight from the burning star
that guides poetic jewels –
here there are no rules:
words can come dropping
fresh, pure, like water –
colourless, rainbowed,
clear as light flowed
to mind and heart
to be bent into art
gently, with love –
for 'here there are no rules'.

2 -   The Sacred Space of the word

Selected, tested, just like a fine
carefully distilled and aged wine;
fitting exactly into one space,
meaning, precisely, and with grace
that which we wish to say
with words of sacred space.
Opening the heart and soul
to music from the inner mind;
turning the eye's beholding
into Words;
the soul's thoughts to sentences,
painting a tale in colour as we write.
How can we live without
that sacred space –
heart fumbles for exact
and careful facets expressing love,
describing faith, praising the great,
with neither paint nor brush
but words, chosen in no great rush
from what the mind skims
from the boiling brain
as feelings flow,as wisdoms grow.
And as we learn to wait in patience by the gate
leading to paradise – the sacred Space of Words.
Teach me how to choose those pearls on silken string,
those sentences to use each one a perfect jewel ,
set where it will glow in the best light
for other souls to see and to set free
a sacred space in life, gems from the brain –
wrought by the burning heart by alchemy of Poet's art
a Sacred Space, indeed!
After A Workshop with Jay Ramsay.

3 - What Poetry Is.

This should be the distillation
of all my lived life,
informing what I write,
birth, death re-birth,
or rather, resurrection.

It should be the knowledge of all years,
shaken and stirred together,
that shapes what I should say,
as I stand on the cusp of agedness.

And it should be the yielding up
of worldliness, of vanity;
the spreading out of charity
whether I like or no.

And it should be recollection
of every love, all pain,
all anxiety and all ill,
transformed into experience,
and used in words to fill
all that I write, all prose,
all poetry, brought to a sweet close.

2004

4 -   Waiting for a Book

I await a book, long looked for,
written of you, and of your friends -
will I hear your song, silver-voiced,
you, sweet-throated, lark-like one?
Or will the critic writer dim
the words you wrote, the words you said –
curb that out-flow of melodic prose
and more melodic verse?
No! in my head I'll hear you.
Sweet Singer, sing again I hear:
my ear is open as my heart
to drink each word, note every phrase,
then stand in wonder, all my days.
As long as I recall, always,
I've wanted this book on my shelves,
a closer, nearer stand
to you, - not that I understand
why your words haunted, helped me –
your thoughts,your opinions, and ideas,
challenged me, made me search again
for what I now believe, and keep, what deny
'Most beautiful of Singers, sing again!'
I wait, impatient,
for this one Book.

5 -   Holding a book

It's not just the words within,
but also the binding:
leather perhaps, or silk,
and the paper -
rice, hand-made,
or a fine linen-wove.
Perhaps there may be pictures,
guarded by slivers
of slim transparency –
gilded edges, letters
worked with great craft,
upon the spine.
Truly a work of art:
all this without the contents!
So, add the genius
of what inspired poets wrote -
the work of art's completed -
sensuous, but cerebral still;
and it's so beautiful!
A pleasure to the eye,
the hand, the heart,
and most of all,
the soul.

2001.

6 - What Was It Worth

And was it worth
the few quid of pay,
a few feet of earth
at the end of the day?

All these white headstones,
graves of the heroes,
scattered like dry bones
stretching away!

Now to those young men
we will pay homage,
who went marching
bright, full of courage,
so handsome and gay:
fewer come home,
so late in the day.

Now they come back
zipped up in body bags
nothing they lack
all wrapped in flags.

Why did they fight
what did they die for?
When was it right
to kill for lie?

So, was it worth
the few quid of pay,
six foot of earth,
at the end of their day.

23rd Feb. 2004.

7 -   News

Always sad news!
radio, papers, television,
full of despair and death,-
and useless death!

Yet there are good things too:
women who work, against all odds,
to help their sisters of another Faith,
who try to heal the wounds of war
ameliorate distress:
the trucks at Bayt Jala
sent by Israeli women
in good faith,
to Palestinian cousins -
singing and weeping with them;
praying together, too,
in the cause of Peace
and Palestinian women who
join with them in woman's faith
in woman's light, and love;
regard Israeli friends as truly friends.
And all around the world
are groups of women,
sending prayers for Peace,
sending all they can to aid
suffering sisters in far lands
where terror reigns -
and they, all unafraid
risk their lives to bring relief-
food medicine and blankets.
These things we do not hear!

When shall we set up schools
to teach our children
their own humanity?
Not how to pass their CSE
but how to be people in the round:
good manners, courtesy and love –
and that great blessing, too,
to understand,
and to respect our differences,
dwell on where we are alike;
then all the world's young citizens may grow
in peace and love for all their fellow-men –
no-one left out or barred -
just one harmony.
Women debating,
not a race to arms but dinner,
health of their husband and their child.
Oh sisters! Join in this the work of prayer,
and put a girdle round the earth
composed of love and empathy -
that place for woman in cosmology –
our secret: unconditional Love!

8 -   The Navajo code breakers

We did not hear your praises sung
in this, our Country, far away;
but on your words our fortunes hung
on many a desperate wartime day.
We call you 'Braves' and brave you were
whose secret language kept each plan,
keeping the enemy in despair,
saving the life of many a man.
And now, before Time takes you all
to new and Happy Hunting Lands
all those remaining can stand tall
as all around your fame resounds.
In England now, we've come to know
how much depended on your word,
reverence and respect we'll show
to every man who spoke the Code.

In WWII, Navajo men risked their lives in order to pass on
information in their own unique language, which they then
encrypted, making it impossible to break.

2005

9 - Reading the White Poem by Jay Ramsay

Reading this poem, comes a plan
scribbled like sea-weed, strung with letters fine
above the ocean's smooth retreating line.
This new song must be made to rhyme and scan
this my newest poem, youngest daughter –
waiting to see what thought may come to hand;
so, while the pebbles scattered on the sand,
this poem was conceived of light on water.

And since I have no photograph to use,
and no photographer to catch the views,
to trap a picture, see it once again,
some muddled images of breaking waves
are seen - up-ended fishing boat
all complete with tackle and with float,
with rags of sea-weed clinging to the staves.
Here is the thunder of the waves
filling at high tide all the open cave –
trapping the loiterer who did not save
himself by hurrying in time to seize
the opportunity to leave the beach,
and so was caught in such a great alarm
before he found a place of safety, calm,
along the cliffs that he had climbed to reach.
Recalling sounds and places that have been
in countryside and seaside, cove and farm,
perfection natural, and man-made calm
are shown again on memory's clear screen.

Along break-waters sea birds sit-
fledged, so the old monks said, from mollusc shells –
from beach to dune imagination dwells,

and back and forth, between, the sand flies flit.
A path of hot sand and of blue sea-grass
leads back to where the lighthouse stands
on rocky headland, above wrecking sands
built straight and white,
of stone and shining brass.

A sky-lark, small but joyous bird
flies up on wings so frail and fine
they scarce can carry melody divine,
whose song of all emotion Shelley heard.

Far down below, and too far out to reach
a human figure, braced against the beach
stands with open arms, extended hands –
inland that figure's seen again,
trudging along the weary, endless road
hot in the sun ,and carrying a load,
dragging his feet along, as if in pain.-
not here the gay abandon of the sea
the fun and laughter of the sunny beach –
even the song of skylarks cannot reach
ears muffled up in such dark misery.

Yet still more pictures come into the mind:
on uplands human hands have piled up high –
a man-made hill that reaches to the sky
to mark a chieftains or priestess's tomb
around the brow of the green hill
ancient people circled it with lines
and still the villagers go up with teigns
to keep it marked and standing clearly still,
while that dark figure that was seen before
now trudging on a black and rain-swilled road,

comes into view once more – born of this land.
Here is the farmer, here the farmer's man,
and here is Herne the Hunter with his hound ;
here still, in secret England, can be found
that ancient deity, the great Green Man.

So far from the white beach this poem's strayed
and soon is lost the path that had been laid
to set the feet upon – the plans once made,
yet ancient spirits still must be obeyed –
and so the depth of England's rural heart is come
where village greens and duck ponds greenly lie.
and every villager who passes by
inspects the traveller with anxious eye –
wondering, that one so far from Home is come!.

10 - Hope Dawning

Towards the dawn I turn
in wonder; wondering
what the full day will bring
will my known world burn?

At noon I see the sun
shining, but for how long?
How soon will clouds of war
render the blue sky dun?

At night I see the stars
and cannot help but think
while on extinction's brink –
why pay to visit Mars?

The papers that I read
all write of bombs and death
why pay to ruin Earth,
when people are in need?

Politicians seem
to think there's need for guns
but we should save our sons-
it's every mothers' dream.

I've dreamed Love shall prevail
above all 'Holy' wars,
and raise a hymn of praise
above all weapons sale!

11 - Forgiveness

Let us seek forgiveness
for without it bread will have no taste,
our money be but 'Faery gold',
our best attempts must fail
because of bitterness.

Let us seek union
with other women, no matter who,
or where, whatever station
Fate has placed them in,
for all our aims are one:
familial safety, food for everyone,
good health, and blankets for the cold.

Let us go hand in hand
begging a pardon for our sisters' plight,
offering amelioration for their lot,
with love – for their concerns are ours-
their children and their men:-

Our likenesses are so much more
than all our differences:
let us then seek grace, and offer up
our understanding
and our love.

2002.

12 - November Influenza

November's shortened day looks cold and grey;
alone and sickly, I keep to my bed
in solitude and silence here I lie
watching the fleeting glimmers of the day
move,silver, on the mountain's wilderness,
should I but gently stir my aching head.
No leaves are left, to rustle on the trees
through thick-glazed windows no sweet songs are heard
from those few birds that choose to winter here.
The rime is on the uplands, chill and sere –
when I was young, there was a cosy fire
made in my room, if ever I was ill:
the crackling flames were company for me,
but central heating offers no such cheer.
Tomorrow I will rise, be well again,
and venture out into the wintry air:
but until then I'll lie and watch the hill
grow dark and sombre, with the ageing year!

29/11/2004

13 - R.S. Thomas, the Bard

Gaunt-thoughted,
this Welsh-speaking,
agnostic, clergyman
supremely commanded
the English language;
so masterfully
made it sing in Welsh.

The heart bleeds
for his waiting, empty ear,
his constant, hopeful,
hopelessness.

May he find rest
amid his green Welsh hills;
solace with a god
who speaks to him;
and peace at last
from desperate searchings;
shelter from grey rain,
and cold wind's atheism,
high valleys' misery.

May he meet with
happy countrymen
who have enough to eat,
and who believe
his fervent musicality
of language –
though it is not their own:
Dear God! May he find love!
2004-02-23

14 - The Searcher

I've searched for you
for many years,
but you elude me,
vanishing, spirit like,
as you always did.
You stopped the
car one day
to show the way
to your museum

We met once, in a park
at your old home,
picking violets.
You met me at your gate
to swing gaily,
as you would a child.

One day you told me
of a programme
on the television.

Ah! But still I search,
reading your poetry,
seeking out your prose,
letters, perhaps
or journals,
if you kept such things.

But one day I shall meet you,
when I least expect,
will waken to that voice
that's shrill but thrilling,
heard inside my head
above Cwm Elan,
laughing at Tan Yr Allt.

And I will know you
with your blazing eyes
bright with some project
for the good of man –
when it's my time to go
where poets dwell,
still making poems,
then I shall meet you –
Ariel!

2002

15 - Shelley at Speed

I imagine you,
Sweetest of singers,
piloting a micro-plane,
thrilling with speed
as you
fly through
the air,
laughing aloud
through clouds.;
shouting joyful stanzas
from a power boat,
as you cry sonnets,
water spraying
from your hair!
And I see you,
most musical of singers,
who sang in Tuscany,
experiencing speed –
that dream of masculinity-
racing a red
Ferrari!

2001

16 - For Stevie Smith

Lady of lively lays
there is no letter
that you could add, or take away
to make your poems better!
With words close as a hazel nut
you paint your canvases
glowing like conker-skin
and encompassing
so much within so little.
Beautiful and brittle,
still as bright today
as when your pen
waved them away.

2001

17 - For a Poet

So you have been swallowed
by that bright water ring
you so much loved,
and suffered for.
Gone beyond bodies now,
Spirit can blend
in fearless laughter;
your voice can sing
in unison with Nature,
and with him whose love
was not the love of women,
but who loved your soul.
You can rise to where the trees
breathe out a cleansing air,
where all your loves and pains are one
and pacified and gone:
no need now for the blame you laid
upon yourself;
your lifted soul will judge life
all its woes and trials and tragedies
joyously rising through the songs you made
to join with whom you truly loved
and truly made
the centre of your life,
outside a poet's fate.
Arising, you will find it's never late
when you have given so much love,
such charity!

K.R. RIP. July 2003

18 - Selina's Cyclsmen

Bright cyclamen against my pale pink wall
The shining gift of friendship in its bloom,
Shapely, petals turning back, and all
the gloss of colour in the winter gloom.
If I should touch the blossoms, they might fall,
so, carefully, I water from below,
and every time I pass them by, I stop,
heartened and cheered by their vivid glow!
The friend who gave them to me's vivid too –
aged in years, but not enthusiasm,
still wearing lovely clothes, she's one whose
life is a work of art and heroism.,
and with a generous and a loving heart.
The flower buds open in my heated room,
and take the shafts of sunlight when it comes,
enhancing beauty in each fragile bloom,
and never trace of languor ever comes
for I am lifted by my friend's panache,
her vibrant nature and her forthright charm.
These cyclamen will one day turn to ash,
her generosity will still live on!

1998

19 - Rosemary

Even you, Shelley, the perfect singer,
could find no words with which to sing
that death, so close to you,
your small, beloved, William.
There fore it seems to make more sense
that I, bereaved, can never bring
my heart or head to tell the tense
and drawn out feelings
that I have for her, my daughter.
I never saw her. No one photographed
her small, pale face for me,
so that forever I could see
what she had looked like – Rosemary!
I have no curl of golden hair,
no small shoe that once she'd wear.
I can wait in peace no more
until I come to find her there
where the young dead grow
into the souls that they were meant to be.
Come, Shelley! Do you sing for me
since I, her mother, cannot sing
for all the tears that memories bring –
sing for my daughter, sing for me!

2001

20 - Bryan's Green finch

You took the tiny heart-pounding thing
into your ample, work-worn hands:
tears in your eyes 'A baby greenfinch
I got it off the dog, poor little thing'.
It had not flown the nest. No doubt
the parents or the other brood
had pushed it out.
'What shall we do – I cannot let it die!'
You said; and many 'phone calls later I
found myself cradling, with great care
the tiny bird, at sixty miles an hour,
to where the only open
'Wild Life Shelter' was, at ten at night,
fearing it may die before we got there.
It was received and numbered.
I gave them cash for bird food,
for I remembered that it must be fed.
The man said 'they usually survive'..
So we drove homeward, hopefully.
Later, I telephoned and heard
our little bird was dead.
'There aren't enough greenfinches in this world'
with tear-bright eyes, was all you said.

Spring.2001.

21 - For John Fox

Chosen with precise clarity
your words are beautifully strung
upon a chain of strong meaning,
of exceptional depth: are hung
upon the web of experience,
always with gentle charity,
most courageously leaning
into the tempest of your thought.
Rare, in these modern days
to find a poet who will use
language carefully selected
from the individual muse;
with every nuance gently caught
polished, faceted, exactly set,
spontaneously, with brimming
emotion; never self-regarding, yet
ever-flowing, whole, from the heart's depth.

The Lapidus Meeting; .Frampton Court, 11/08/2004

22 - My Sisters first Ball

I remember you
in your blue satin gown,
tying your curls
with velvet ribbon bow,
spinning round to show
the silver threads
at the 'sweetheart neck'.
Pointing the toe
of your silver shoe,
sheening in the gas-lamp's glow.
I remember your first dance
Do you? It was so long ago.
So long ago!
And you have gone before me
to that far place
where I can't see
the gas light glow on silver lace
your satin gown,
your silver shoe
or ribboned hair.
excited face.
But I know you are there.
Do you hear me –
hear the thoughts
and memories –
a sister's love,
that never dies,
calling, in the silver night
in moonlight, starlight, candlelight-
remembering that happy night
of your first Ball!

Remembering 1947.

23 - The Offical Letter

Just a paper in an envelope,
ordinary and bright. I thought it junk mail;
I was shocked, on opening it,
To see your name there –
'The Late', 'Deceased'.

Your name.
Money you had left to me -
not for my use,
but for debts your husband made,
that I must now discharge.
Not that I wanted money –
But I had not seen you laid to rest,
as any sister should.

I hold this paper,
counting, as one would,
to share it all around.
But you are dead – you are gone,
never more to telephone
say 'Happy Birthday'
'Happy Christmas, Tish!'

So this paper made me cry-
not for the money,
which is not for me,
but for my loss of you!
Seeing in my mind your face,
pale, eyes shut.

Imagining you there
as you were,
dressed in your black gown,
with your tired, pale face,
as if you were asleep - not there:

'Like looking into a black hole'
your daughter said
I wish it had been me instead,
mourning you there -
because I loved you
my sister , always there-
but you've gone now -

I don't want the debts paid,
I want you back,
not dressed in black,
but all in Light.
Your eyes bright
as they always were

Oh God!
Make us two whole again.
Two women, as one, sister.
As I type
The programme says
'Word is saving Maureen'
How I wish it could
and wish it would -
my sister!

2001

24 - Moonrise

She rises gently on the hill,
letting her golden touch dispel
the dark of evening with her rays
glowing amid the clouds,
the moon – inviolate, in spite of man!
She shines, incandescent
glorious in her ascent
who could intruded on her face-
what members of the human race
could travel there, to that cold shore!
Still and beautiful she watches
throughout the dark night of our world
lifting all colour from the grasses -
radiant, perfect, unmolested, chill –
The Lady Moon, a huntress still!

2003

25 - Dawn

The light is growing:
intense and urgent on the hill
where gradual colour seeps
into the trees and grass,
and birds awake to sing.
It is the light, glowing
joyously into the heart
heralding one more day of bright
and hopeful life;
warming the flower buds
to blowing bloom,
defrosting frozen hearts,
dispelling gloom,
illuminating all the world
but, most of all,
so brightly
irradiating
the soul!

2004

26 - Empty Space

And so I ask if you can see the space
just halfway down, below my face –
an empty region, cold and grey –
it's where my heart has gone away.
If you look hard enough, you'll see
the place where my heart used to be –
it's dark there, where it once was light,
that's when I thought it glad and bright.
now there's not a single token
See! My heart is lost and broken:
I thought it strong, but then one day
a thief came by and took away
the broken heart – he said he'd mend it
he didn't say he'd bruise and bend it-
now I'll never get it back,
the place it left is dead and black –
you can see the empty place,
just halfway down, below my face.

2001

27 - Any Wife to any Husband

Winter came early;
no frost outside;
only in my heart.
You'd think my love
would melt the cold
but no. Not so.
Love froze; is smothered,
for respect is lost
with this one more woe.
Crushed like a book-worm
is the love within
and only bitterness
the lees of trust
remain,
hauntingly present
tainting everything
And yet I cook and clean,
make conversation,
coffee, meals.
and all the while,
love freezes -
Iced by your contempt.

2003

28 - I was once told

I once was told
the sweetest love
remains unconsummated.
Maybe that is true:
the rub and soil
of every day
may dim the gold
of lovers' joy
with commonplace.
Not many poets words
record the socks
darned by their wives-
for their imagined lives
are lived elsewhere.
Beatrice did not mend
Alighieri's cloak,
nor did she send
his worn shoes
to the cobbler,
when he had
walked through worlds,
and Juliet was not
her Romeo's laundry maid. -
for soon would magic fade,
and humdrum take the place
of high Romance.

Thus it is better far to dream
than to encompass dreams –
make them come true.
Love then is ever young,
Love knows not age,
the Loved One does not change
or bright dreams fade.
The Love most poignant
still unconsummated lies -
so I was told,
and grows not old.

2000

29 - What Plato Taught

Plato taught that we seek Love
more lovely than the Love we know,
the other portion of ourselves –
existing somewhere.
Sadly but few will find it so.
Yet still we search,
and in that searching find
new loveliness of face or mind,
of intellect or soul.
Then why not love
those too rare Loves
seeking the other half of us,
our soul-mate lover
who will perfection be?
Seeking and loving, so we grow –
for Love but adds to Love,
nor takes from any other love
because another soul is fair
of form, intelligence, or grace.
In every one we love there's one to love,
for every spirit is a part of God –
whatever we perceive that god to be –
and offerings to God are always free –
a talent, gift of grace – humanity.
Love added to another grows apace,
giving to Loved, and Lover, endless grace!

2001

30 - A Shell from Greece

I hold a sea-shall
brought from the Isles of Greece;
it does not sound the sea-
delicate, it could not
convey the waves.
Yet, in my hand
it's fragile, warm,light
and it is well.

This token of deep peace
that was brought home to me
from a Greek beach, so hot,
where water laves
and laps the fishing keels
in sunlight bright.

And still its spell
seems only to increase
friend's thoughtfulness for me -
it does hold a spell:
friendship and peace,
a kindly thought for me
from those blue waves,
that sing of peace!

1999.

31 - Going Home to the Cotswold

I shall go back to where the Avon flows,
silver in moonshine, blue beneath the sky
as sun rides high; to where the blossoms hand,
on apple, plum,, pear, damson and cherry;
where green fields climb the summit of the Hill
to standing stones, set in antiquity.
I'll visit the church whose steeple rises
pointing ever up, carrying the prayers
of countless village generations,
and a myriad of meditations,
as yew trees bend low down above the graves
where village yeomen lie, interred in peace.

This place was blessed with books from ancient times –
here I learned their worth; in green groves growing
on Worcestershire's rich earth I learned to love
both poetry and souls. I'll come again
to find my old content of summer days
on tussocks of soft hay;
the simple swing where all the day I'd play
dreaming and singing every song I knew
or made, among surrounding morning flowers –
wet with the dew, or dried by the noon-sun
opening wide rich petals - the poppies
dark-tasselled, red, and the mock-orange sweet.

One day I shall return, my memories meet.
I'll ride the lanes by trap or on horse-back,
braving the tractor and the braying ass,
along the winding ways to villages
shaded by tall trees in ranks that straggle
over the ancient banks and mounting steps,

ale houses, farmsteads, barns. Epitome
of Worcestershire and Home!
Home to the tack-room, stable, apple store
fruit-packing shed, and pump - whose hollow, sunk,
caused chaos, made me jump, heart-beating fast –
at thoughts of where the well reached ever down-
my own idea of hell! Yet softened there
by beauty all around me, fresh and free:
now marred, yet still I'll go back there, come the day,
back to where I knew true peace and beauty,
back to my beloved my cottage home.

Light filtered through the window pane
of the oak-panelled room that was my own;
with polished floor-boards and a cosy rug,
a marble wash-stand and a pretty jug;
excitement of a candle's gentle light-
no other lamp, when I had said goodnight,
but candle stick and gently burning flame.
The smell of beeswax and of apples came
from the oak panels all around the room –
apples were stored there, curtains shut for gloom,
before the advent of a family
seeking a refuge from the noise of war:
and I had never known such peace before!

So early scenes of childhood have been blessed
with love and light and joy, at my behest,
for I soon had the kind old man in thrall –
patient, indulgent, and prepared to fall
beneath the spell a little girl could wield
upon a man who never had a child.
And I could roam the gardens all the day,
and swing beneath the apple boughs, and play.

A blessed childhood, safe from war and strife,
a soft beginning for a harsher life!
In that bright cottage room I learned to read,
to study pictures, and to take some heed
of beauty, natural or made by art,
fearlessly opening my infant heart.
So many happy summers came and passed
before I left that magic place at last
for London's duller skies and dusty street
where bloomed no buttercups or meadowsweet
to play amongst, and there no apples kept-
was it great wonder that I often wept?

But life goes on, whatever fate may throw,
whether a child is happy, safe, or no.

And Oh! So often in my mind returning
to village life and cottage fires returning,
dejected by the lack of trees and sky,
seeing no birds but pigeons flutter by,
I took to going back, in mind and soul,
to where that good old man had made Life whole
for me, a city child, for safety sent
to where the apple tree and lilac lent
sweet fragrance to the waking day,
and Bredon Hill was background to my play.
and that small panelled room with apple scent
was all my world, and all my safe content.

Yet Life would not stand still, nor Time delay
because a foolish girl would stop and play.
Youth came and went, with love and toil,
for toil we must and Love will ever spoil
the innocence of childhood's open heart –
once given, ever bruised, is loving's part!

In dreary London with its leaden skies
I lived and worked, with those un-severed ties.
But one day it was time to come again
to Cotswold, though not back to that green lane,
where childhood's memory lives and laughs –
Time only ever pays us back by halves!

Yet, here I am, and here I daily trust
in Gloucestershire's kind soil to lay my dust;
come home at last, not to my apple-room,
but to a place where I can see the gloom
creep slowly over steep Leckhampton Hill
and watch the moon, leaf-framed in glory still.

I had my youthful dreams of Life's vast stage,
but now have found peace sweeter, with old age:
quiet to live, to read and write, and hear
sweet music and kind words upon my ear
from treasured friends, with loved ones by my side –
to live in peaceful Beauty and abide
for some years more yet: time to make my soul
a fit receptacle for Heaven's dole.

For long years I have toiled to find this Peace,
how blessed it is now to cease
in Cotswold's air, in time, to breathe my last,
where graceful trees long shadows gently cast.

One asked his name be writ in water –I
need no such epitaph when I shall die:
Cotswold will hold me, Cotswold be my bed,
and no grey stone shall mark my sleeping head!

2003.

32 - End notes

Sylvia Charlewood is a wife, mother, and grandmother who has written poetry all her life. In her seventieth decade, she has decided to make a selection to offer to others. Her poems are simple and usually refer to the small, daily happenings in life. Her great love is for the work of P B Shelley, whose wonderful lyrical poetry has inspired her since she was a young child.

www.ingramcontent.com/pod-product-compliance
Lightning Source LLC
Chambersburg PA
CBHW071748020426
42331CB00008B/2220